# LET'S · BRING · BACK

*A Journal*

# FOR THE MUSINGS, NOTIONS, & REMINISCENCES
## OF MODERN NOSTALGISTS

LESLEY M. M. BLUME

CHRONICLE BOOKS
SAN FRANCISCO

# INTRODUCTION

IN MANY WAYS, it appears that modern life conspires to keep us from having adventures, whether grand or small. It has become, for instance, increasingly difficult to leave the work e-mail unanswered—even if it comes in at midnight—or to squirrel away the time to host even the most modest of gatherings in our homes. In other words, modern living affords us little space in which to disconnect, quietly *imagine*, and conjure up novel experiences for ourselves.

Now, in bygone eras, there was work, of course—and plenty of it. Historically speaking, leisure time was until recently a foreign concept to most of our planet's inhabitants. So, it's particularly ironic that our predecessors were so superior to us when it came to cultivating countless hobbies, amusements, outings, and other such delights to entertain themselves when the working day was done. These ancestors instinctively understood that their diversions weren't necessarily frivolous; rather, they guaranteed a certain quality of life. Midnight suppers, ladies' luncheons, and dinner parties weren't chores; they were pleasures. People made the time to do such things because those rituals and events brought something vital and meaningful into their lives.

How can we rediscover this practice of leisure—and by extension, a sense of joy, wonderment, and intimate connection with the world around us? This quest is the central purpose of *Let's Bring Back*, whose first volume was an encyclopedia celebrating hundreds of forgotten-yet-delightful objects, pastimes, and ideas. The *Let's Bring Back* journal aims to continue that fine celebration and hopes to inspire its owner to cultivate a roster of adventures in his or her life, using the nostalgia-inspired ideas on its pages.

Saturated with whimsy and curiosity, these cues are at once sensory and intellectual, sophisticated and childish. They remind us to take the time—as our forebears did—to go on a winter picnic (very *Doctor Zhivago*–chic); host a Belle Epoque color-themed dinner party; take an evening stroll through the neighborhood instead of watching bad television; and set yourself apart by sporting a slinky set of Rita Hayworth-esque evening gloves.

As you embark on these divine adventures, make sure to record your experiences here in these pages. After all, at heart, *Let's Bring Back* has always been about preserving the experience of artful living. The first step in doing so is keeping a faithful record of yourself.

And, of course, anyone who follows the *Let's Bring Back* doctrine of living will boast a legacy worthy of celebration for decades to come.

Wear an old-fashioned string of pearls.
Like affectations, faux pearls become real
as you wear them.

Watch a black-and-white Fred Astaire film. He was everything a man should be: smooth, debonair, intelligent, adult, witty, and wise.

Buy a bouquet of Bachelor's Buttons—a far more charming name for cornflowers, which of course have nothing to do with corn at all.

No swimming costume is complete without
a bright bathing cap! Buy one. Those flower-
covered 1960s ones always looked so cheerful.

Use the word *becoming* again.

As in: "That color is very becoming on you."

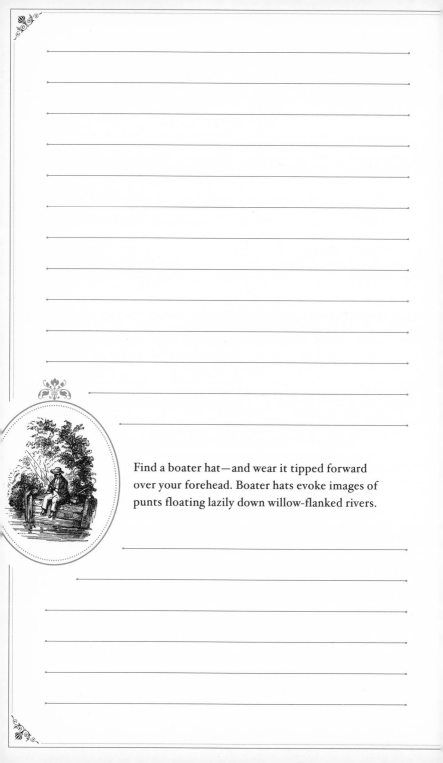

Find a boater hat—and wear it tipped forward over your forehead. Boater hats evoke images of punts floating lazily down willow-flanked rivers.

Paste bookplates into your favorite books. Bookplates tell their own story; therefore, a book that sports one tells two stories for the price of one.

Tuck a gardenia behind your ear and wear it to dinner. Such a flourish is both innocent and sensual at the same time.

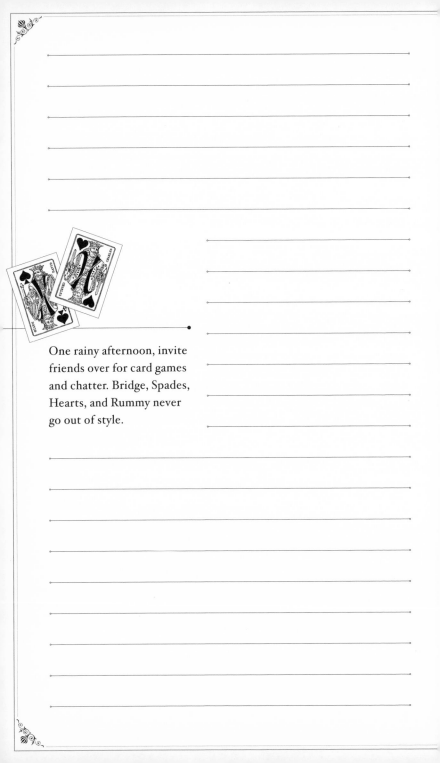

One rainy afternoon, invite friends over for card games and chatter. Bridge, Spades, Hearts, and Rummy never go out of style.

Wrap your holiday presents in brown paper and twine. It's a democratic and mysterious approach to gift wrapping: There could be anything from a diamond necklace to a slab of fish inside.

Wear your hair braided and wound into a bun at the nape of your neck. Such arrangements can look like elaborately wrought works of art.

Have a stack of lovely calling cards made — and then pay a call. In Victorian times, calling cards became an inspired art form and had their own coded language.

P. F. — Congratulations *(pour féliciter)*

P. R. — Thank you *(pour remercier)*

P. C. — Condolences *(pour condoléance)*

P. F. N. A. — Happy New Year *(pour féliciter Nouvel An)*

P. P. C. — Taking leave *(pour prendre congé)*

P. P. — Introducing yourself *(pour présenter)*

Throw a party and build a glistening champagne tower. Popular in the 1920s, such towers are still the prettiest monuments to decadence.

Start a black-paged clippings album in which you tape your latest snipped-out newspaper and magazine mentions—*très* Holly Golightly.

Amaze and amuse your friends with a color-themed dinner-party menu. One historical "red" supper included cherry soup, roast beef with beets, tomato salad, and raspberry sherbet with ripe strawberries.

Script a love letter, preferably with a quill and ink. Let's bring back other courtship rituals too, such as love notes, delivered flowers, mix tapes, and the like.

Take a note from the Victorians and host an afternoon croquet match in your backyard. It's also a wonderfully irreverent way to spend an evening, when played indoors using empty champagne bottles as stakes.

Buy a bouquet of daisies for your kitchen
table; they're the most innocent and cheerful
of flowers, too-often overlooked these days.

Spend the night dining and dancing—preferably the fox-trot or the Charleston in a palm-filled nightclub with zebra-print walls and a discreet little black telephone on each table.

Write in this diary every day, so you'll have a record of your youthful adventures. As an Oscar Wilde character once said, "I never travel without my diary. One should always have something sensational to read in the train."

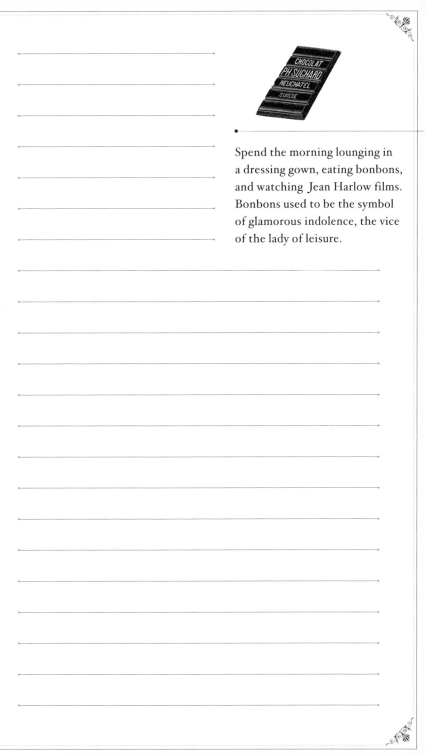

Spend the morning lounging in a dressing gown, eating bonbons, and watching Jean Harlow films. Bonbons used to be the symbol of glamorous indolence, the vice of the lady of leisure.

Time for a holiday: Bring a nécessaire, lap robe, and traveling trunks, of course. Traveling was once considered a glamorous event—and still should be.

Take an evening stroll around your
neighborhood; it's such a civilized
after-dinner occupation.

Purchase several pairs of brightly colored
elbow gloves. Smart midcentury women used
them to chicly elevate even the plainest little
black dresses.

Design a family crest, and put whatever
you like on it—from lions and dragons
to the family Labrador.

Invest in some fake vomit, whoopee cushions,
and other similarly spirited accoutrements.

Carry a lovely handheld fan. In bygone eras, wielders of such fans used them to speak without words; for example, twirling the fan in the left hand meant "We are being watched."

- • • Placing your fan near your heart = *I love you.*
- • • A closed fan resting on the right eye = *When can I see you?*
- • • A half-closed fan pressed to the lips = *You may kiss me.*
- • • Touching the tip of the fan with a finger = *I wish to speak to you.*
- • • Letting the fan rest on the right cheek = *Yes.*
- • • Letting the fan rest on the left cheek = *No.*
- • • Dropping the fan = *We will be friends.*
- • • Fanning slowly = *I am married.*
- • • Fanning quickly = *I am engaged.*
- • • Carrying an open fan in the left hand = *Come and talk to me.*
- • • Twirling the fan in the right hand = *I love another.*
- • • Twirling the fan in the left hand = *We are being watched.*
- • • Shutting a fully open fan slowly = *I promise to marry you.*
- • • Drawing the fan across the eyes = *I am sorry.*
- • • Opening a fan wide = *Wait for me.*

For a delightful Sunday morning breakfast, make Fat Rascals and ham. Serve them with gooseberry jam, of course. Fat Rascals were once Theodore Roosevelt's favorite biscuit.

**FAT RASCALS**

4 cups of flour
1 teaspoon of salt
¼ cup of sugar
4 teaspoons of baking powder

1½ cups of butter
1 pound of dried currants
1 cup of milk

*Sift the flour with the salt, sugar, and baking powder. Mix well. Cut in the butter. Then stir in the dried currants. Mix well again and add the milk, little by little. With each addition, mix with a fork until a soft dough forms. Roll the dough approximately ½ inch thick on a lightly floured board. Use a 2-inch-round cutter to shape the biscuits. Bake biscuits on an ungreased cookie sheet until nicely browned. Bake in a hot (450 degrees F) oven about 12 minutes. When done, remove from oven, split and butter each biscuit, and serve piping hot. Makes approximately two dozen.*

Print out your photographs and put them in an album. Someday, this will be a lovely way to revisit a wedding, a voyage, or a naughty Sunday afternoon spent in bed.

Swap out your ballpoint pen for a fountain pen—or better yet, a quill and ink. Never sign an important document with cheap ink, especially a contract.

Give your most adored friends a handful of old-fangled friendship pins. These elementary-school pleasures get attached to your shoelaces for the whole world to see.

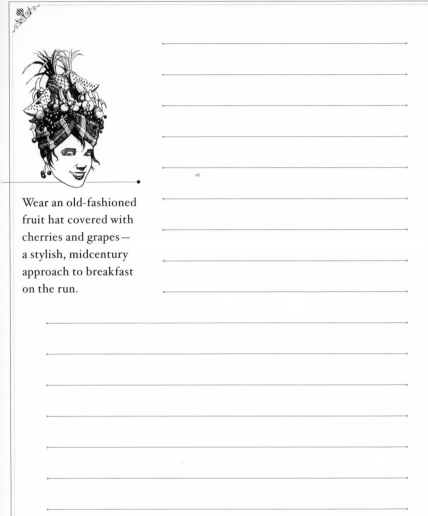

Wear an old-fashioned fruit hat covered with cherries and grapes — a stylish, midcentury approach to breakfast on the run.

Designate Thursday night as game night: Scrabble, Bridge, Poker, Trivial Pursuit, and beyond. Game nights used to serve as wonderful occasions to get soused and gossip.

Host a pretty garden party. Ask the ladies to wear wide-brimmed hats and the men to sport jaunty straw fedoras; pass out cucumber sandwiches and punch.

Forget the weary cosmopolitan; order a gimlet instead. They've long been a great favorite among Southern *grandes dames*.

**GIMLET**

½ jigger Burrough's Plymouth Gin
½ jigger Rose's Lime Juice Cordial

*Stir and serve in a glass over ice.*

The next rainy afternoon, curl up with a book of J. D. Salinger stories; spend some time with the Glass family, Holden Caulfield, and *Little Shirley Beans* again.

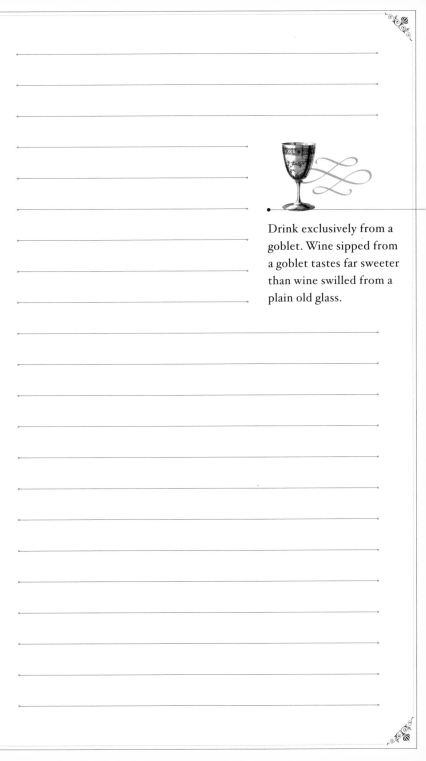

Drink exclusively from a goblet. Wine sipped from a goblet tastes far sweeter than wine swilled from a plain old glass.

Train yourself to become a *grande dame*. They used to be pillars of chic society and still should be.

Make old-fashioned griddlecakes for breakfast. After all, what could be more delightful than having cake first thing in the morning?

Buy a guest book for your foyer;
after all, a house needs a diary too.

Acquire a small stack of dainty handkerchiefs: They help you look more contrite and convincing on the witness stand.

Savor the sage bon mots of midcentury costume designer Edith Head. "You can have anything in life if you dress for it," she once wrote—and she was right.

Give your husband, boyfriend, father, or brother a debonair fedora. There was a time when no self-respecting man would leave the house without one.

Wear a colorful silk headscarf to brunch. They're very Jackie-Kennedy-and-Lee-Radziwell-in-Capri, and an excellent alternative to pulling your hair back into a stringy ponytail.

Learn how to make colonial hot toddies. They're the real cure for the common cold, and therefore a reasonable excuse to stay drunk all winter long.

| HOT TODDY | 1 tablespoon honey |
| | ¾ cup tea |
| | 2 shots brandy |
| | 1 slice lemon |

*Brew tea and fill a tall glass ¾ full. Mix in honey and brandy shots, and add the lemon slice.*

Beekeeping, butterfly collecting, scrapbooking: Start a pleasing, old-fashioned hobby today.

Take up hula-hooping.
Even the ancient
Greeks used grapevine
hoops for exercise.

Go ice-skating—and then host an after-skating supper.
White figure skates and a red plaid cape make a smashing
skating ensemble; hot soup and mulled wine warm you
up afterward.

## A Supper After a Skating Party

**Hot Buttered Rum**

**Old-Fashioned Vegetable Soup**

**Crusty French Bread**

**Mixed Green Salad**

**Cranberry Cheese Cupcakes**

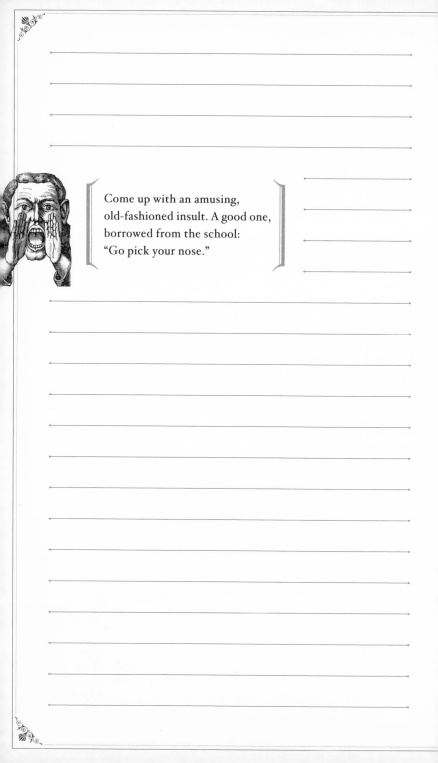

Come up with an amusing, old-fashioned insult. A good one, borrowed from the school: "Go pick your nose."

Another juvenile delight: Buy a bag of jawbreakers. Candy tinged with danger—what could be more enticing to a kid?

Teach yourself how to jitterbug. This crazy
dance likely burns ten times the calories of
a stint on the elliptical.

Wear jodhpurs to lunch—even if you've never ridden a horse. The best part of the equestrian lifestyle has always been the fashion. Jodhpurs are, of course, always best accessorized with a gin and tonic.

Serve juleps to afternoon visitors. Note that they must be served in silver julep cups; otherwise, there's no point.

Wear kitten heels when you go out shopping.
The trademark shoe of Audrey and Jackie,
they're feminine without being torturous.

Watch *La Dolce Vita* again.
The ghost-hunting-in-a-
crumbling-Italian-villa scene
epitomizes glamour.

Form an old-style ladies' club.
They need not be polite affairs.
Just remember that women who
band together get things done.

Learn the language of flowers. To declare love,
give tulips. To declare war, give peonies — they
meant "anger" to the Victorians.

A SHORT LIST OF TODAY'S COMMONLY AVAILABLE FLOWERS
AND THEIR VICTORIAN MEANINGS:

Amaryllis = *pride, haughtiness*
Carnation = *disdain*
Crocus = *youth*
Hyacinth = *constancy*
Jasmine = *amiability*
Lavender = *distrust*
Lilac = *first love*
Lily of the Valley = *modesty*
Peony = *anger*
Rose, red = *beauty and love*
Rose, white = *not looking for love*
Rose, yellow = *jealousy*
Tulip = *declaration of love*
Violet = *modest worth*

Teach yourself Latin.
It is the root of all
romance languages,
and speaking it will
make you seem like
the smartest belle at
the ball.

Play a match of lawn tennis.
Make sure to wear crisp whites
and drink a Pimm's cocktail in
between every game.

Turn your den into a library: A perfect spot for an after-dinner brandy and philosophical discussion.

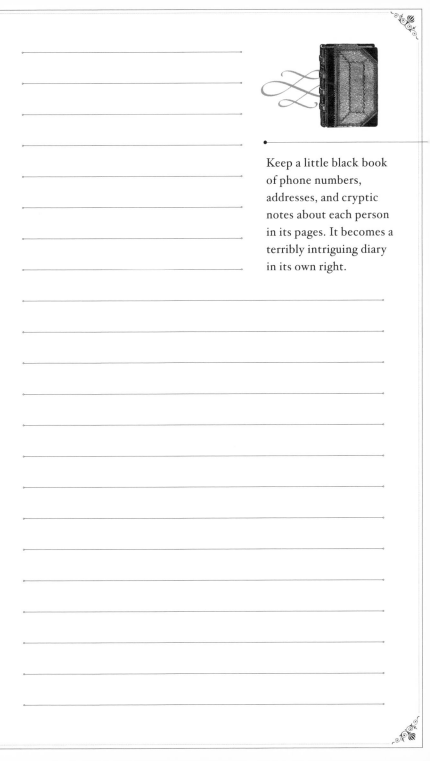

Keep a little black book of phone numbers, addresses, and cryptic notes about each person in its pages. It becomes a terribly intriguing diary in its own right.

Head to the flea market and buy
a charming old locket. They used
to be handy for carrying photos,
locks of hair—and even poison.

Learn lost saloon vocabulary. A *finger* means a shot
the width of a finger; "on the arm" means a free drink.

Use the word *lousy*. As in, "I got a lousy deal," or
"Her hands were lousy with rocks"—a contribution
by the great Holden Caulfield.

Have luncheon with a dear friend. "Lunch" is something you grab, but "luncheon" is a civilized experience.

**CHOCOLATE
MALTED**

1½ ounces chocolate syrup
3 scoops vanilla ice cream
5½ ounces cold milk
1 heaping tablespoon malted milk powder

*Place all ingredients in a blender and
blend until smooth; pour into a chilled
tall glass and top with whipped cream.
Serve with two straws.*

Share a malted with
your sweetie. In the
1950s, they were
invariably served with
two straws for sharing.

Leave the GPS behind and take a map on your next cross-country adventure. They are transportable works of art; foldable adventures; infinite possibility on paper.

Spend Sunday evening watching madcap
old Marx Brothers films. You'll spend the
whole following week in an exceedingly
irreverent mood.

Throw a masquerade ball.
All you need is a big room,
plenty of masks—*et voilà!*
Instant intrigue.

Send a message in a bottle.
The finder will likely never
forget it—such things seem
heaven-sent.

Host an Astor-style midnight birthday supper: a feast that begins at the stroke of midnight, and a delectable way to usher in your next year of life.

Take a milk bath. Once the cornerstone of the pampered lady's beauty regime, they gave glow to the hides of Cleopatra, Queen Elizabeth I, and countless sassy Ziegfeld chorus girls.

**MILK BATH**

*Add 2 to 4 cups of milk or buttermilk to a warm bath, soak for 20 minutes or so, and scrub your skin with a washcloth in soft, circular motions. When you are finished, rinse off with water and supposedly you will be as soft as a baby's bottom.*

Use the amusing old phrase "Mind your own beeswax"—a far chicer way of saying "Butt out" or "Mind your own damn business."

Make a model airplane
and hang it from your
ceiling. It will remind
you that, at any moment,
you could take off on
an adventure.

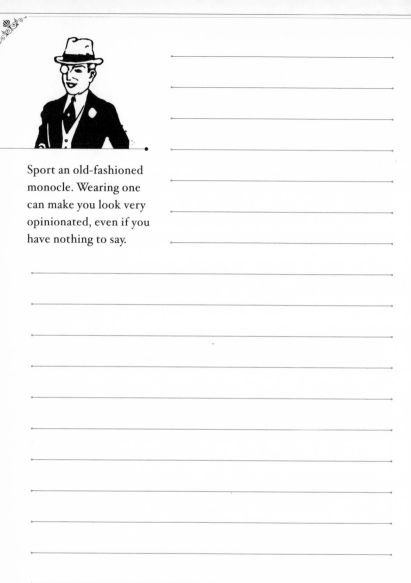

Sport an old-fashioned monocle. Wearing one can make you look very opinionated, even if you have nothing to say.

Monogram the lining
of your coat, like our
grandmothers used
to do. They give the
garment *presence*.

Learn the monthly names for the moon. January brings with it the Wolf Moon; July offers up the Thunder Moon.

Paint a mural on your dining room wall:
Depict your favorite scene from history,
poetry, or fiction.

An evening of entertainment: Give a little music recital at your home. Before the days of radio and television, piano or harp skills were considered mandatory for ladies of good breeding.

Serve old-fashioned Neapolitan ice cream for dessert. Strawberry, vanilla, and chocolate side by side: This combination of colors should be made into the flag of some languorous, pleasure-oriented country.

Cultivate an air of mystery.
It is the root of allure—just
ask Garbo and Dietrich.

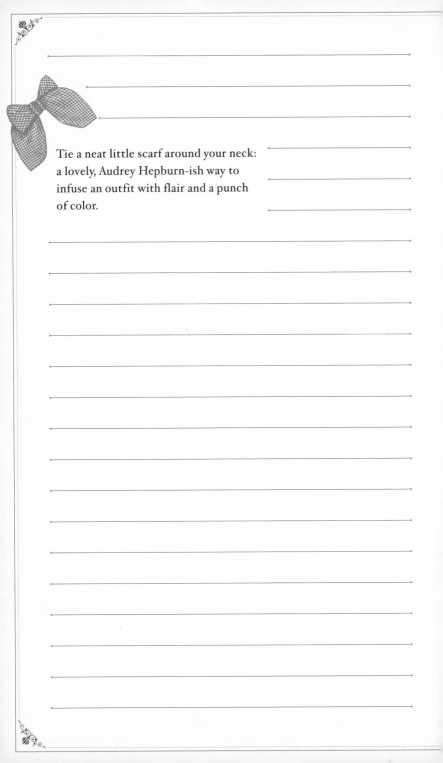

Tie a neat little scarf around your neck: a lovely, Audrey Hepburn-ish way to infuse an outfit with flair and a punch of color.

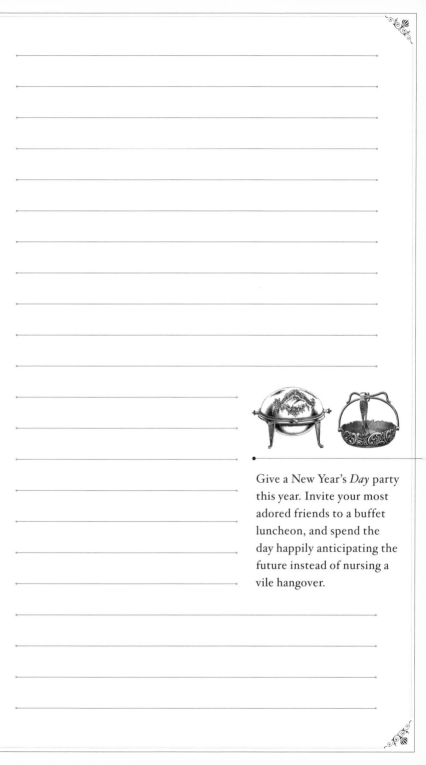

Give a New Year's *Day* party this year. Invite your most adored friends to a buffet luncheon, and spend the day happily anticipating the future instead of nursing a vile hangover.

Wear a nightcap with tassels: It's very Scrooge-chic. Such caps deserve a backdrop of old-guard velvet bed curtains, a bed warmer, and, of course, a bedroom fireplace.

Watch a handful of 1950s sci-fi B movies.
Their effects are often as amusing as their titles.

Go on a date to the opera—wearing an opera cape and opera gloves, and toting opera glasses.

Build a goldfish-and-lily-filled pond. It will be like having a live Matisse painting in your backyard.

Use oversize cutlery—it will give your guests the sensation of dining with the Mad Hatter in *Alice's Adventures in Wonderland*.

Have your children's portraits painted—perhaps in profile, à la the Medicis. Unlike staged mall shots, someone may actually want these paintings later.

Twirl a parasol on your shoulder in the summer sun.
They're such pretty practicalities; women in bygone
eras knew that it was wise to shade their beauty.

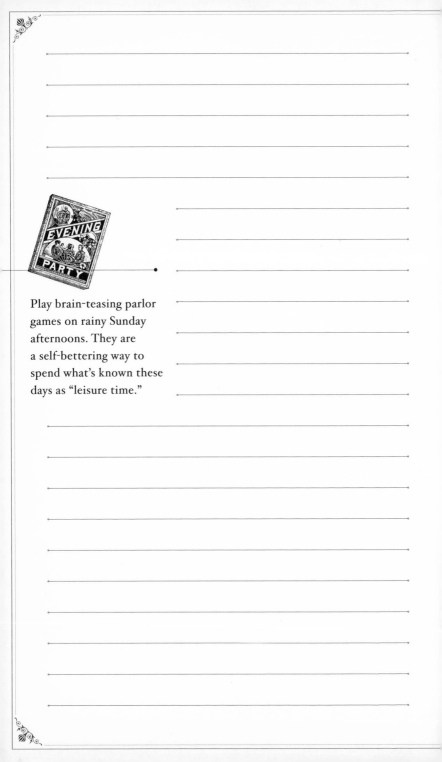

Play brain-teasing parlor games on rainy Sunday afternoons. They are a self-bettering way to spend what's known these days as "leisure time."

Find your patron saint. There are some highly specific ones. A hairdresser, for example, finds herself under the protection of Saint Cosmas; beekeepers, on the other hand, are shielded by Saint Bernard.

Perfect your penmanship. Like good posture, it's an old-guard indicator of elegance. Plus, it's easier than you might think to "invent" individualistic, pretty handwriting.

Wear old-fashioned penny loafers. Have good luck at your feet all day long.

Use the old word *persnickety* more often. It's very fun to say, although its contemporary synonyms are as well: "nitpicky," "fussy," and "finicky."

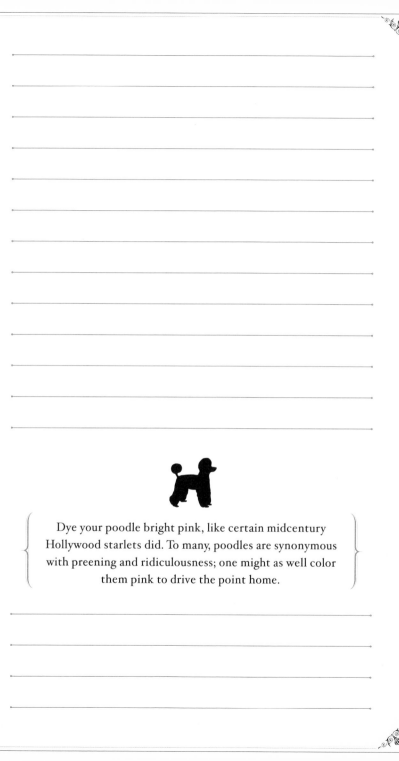

Dye your poodle bright pink, like certain midcentury Hollywood starlets did. To many, poodles are synonymous with preening and ridiculousness; one might as well color them pink to drive the point home.

Memorize and recite your favorite poem.
Poetry is a dying art; we must all do our
part to keep it alive and well.

---

*You say poems never went out of style;*
*I say that you're living in denial.*

Wear polka dots.
They're old-fashioned
but cheerful—good for
a Monday-blues dress.

Send postcards with scalloped edges during your next holiday. They are emblems of faraway adventure, as are memento stickers for your traveling trunks.

Flout a vintage punch bowl at your next fete. They are the Lolitas of serving ware: Filled with pink party punch, they look dainty and sweet and innocent, but portend all sorts of naughty behavior.

• • •———————————————————————————

Read aloud after dinner, preferably fireside. The Sherlock Holmes tales make particularly fetching material for such recitals.

Serve recipes named after royalty. A regal menu: Oysters Rockefeller for an appetizer (after all, Americans have their royalty too); Beef Wellington for the main course; and Strawberries Romanov for dessert.

Reacquaint yourself with the Roman
and Greek gods. They were always up
to something naughty, and their antics
prove endlessly entertaining.

Roller-skate to work.
Those old-fashioned
white skates with red
laces and little keys
were devastatingly chic.

Watch Rosalind Russell in *His Girl Friday*, in which she plays wisecracking ace reporter Hildy Johnson. This film should be mandatory viewing material for feisty young girls and all aspiring journalists.

Instead of a book club, host a salon in your parlor, at which you discuss the issues of the moment. For centuries, private salons served as forums for the exchange of ideas — or a place for people to pick up a few when they were in short supply.

Wear satin evening slippers out on the town. Each pair exudes the promise of dancing-until-dawn, and the most exquisite hangover the next morning.

Use scented ink when scripting your next letter. It makes letter writing even more personalized, as a perfumed extension of yourself.

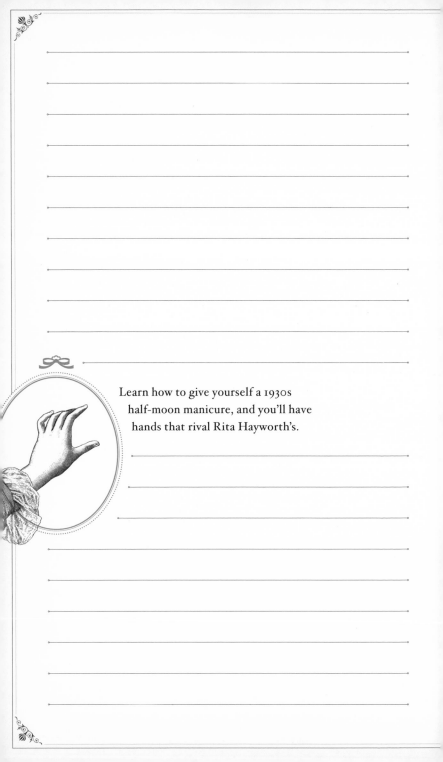

Learn how to give yourself a 1930s
half-moon manicure, and you'll have
hands that rival Rita Hayworth's.

Make a shoo-fly pie for your next family picnic. Invented by the early settlers of Pennsylvania Dutch country, these pies are just as delectable today.

**SHOO-FLY PIE**

1 cup flour
¾ cup brown sugar
1 heaping tablespoon Crisco
1 cup King Syrup
1 teaspoon baking soda

¾ cup boiling water
1 beaten egg
One 10-inch uncooked pie shell

*Preheat oven to 375°F. Mix flour, brown sugar, and shortening into crumbs. Split the crumb mixture in half. Set one half aside for crumbs.*

*Pour the King Syrup in the other half of the crumb mixture. Mix the baking soda in the boiling water. When this fizzes, pour on top of the King Syrup/crumb mixture. If the soda water doesn't fizz, you didn't get your water hot enough or your baking soda is bad. Dump out water and try again. Pie won't rise if it doesn't fizz. Add 1 beaten egg. Mix with fork.*

*Pour in unbaked pie shell. If you don't want to make your own shell, just use one of those fold-out Pillsbury ones. Top with crumbs. Bake in preheated oven for 10 minutes. Without opening the door, turn oven down to 350°F. Bake an additional 30–40 minutes.*

ANOTHER VITAL BUT UNMENTIONED INGREDIENT:
BUZZING FLIES TO SHOO AWAY.

Throw silver streamers on New Year's Eve. The sight of a room absolutely strewn with shimmering silver is a lovely way to herald the new year.

Use the word *spectacles* instead of *glasses*.
No one can deny that "glasses" sounds nerdy,
while "spectacles" sounds charming.

Banish the linoleum pool shed and erect a striped poolside cabana in your backyard. They're like pleasing little temples honoring the French Riviera and the Lido de Venezia in the 1920s.

Wear "Sunday Best" clothing on that day, even if you're the least religious person on the planet. Doing so counterbalances the inanity of Casual Fridays.

Harbor superstitions about black cats, walking under ladders, Friday the 13th, and so on. We're so thumpingly rational and sensible these days—we need some spooky silliness in our lives.

Practice good table manners.
In today's society, it's practically
acceptable to let food fall out of
your mouth onto the plate.

Befriend your tailor and visit him or her often. In the old days, buying new dresses meant fittings — even for nightgowns. Our grandmothers knew what they were doing: After all, a gifted tailor flatters your physical assets and helps mask your flaws.

Make time for teatime again. Dreary afternoon Starbucks runs are not the same thing.

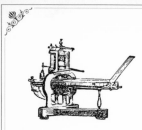

Send an old-fashioned telegram. They're much chicer than a text message; they become great keepsakes and *objets d'art*.

Create themed rooms in your home: the red room, the garden room, the safari room—whatever you fancy. Having a house with the usual bits and bobs ("living room," "dining room," etc.) is dull, dull, dull.

Give traditional anniversary gifts each year: They're open to all sorts of creative interpretation. The fourth anniversary calls for silk: Why not go parachuting together? There is nothing more celebratory than the sight of red parachute silk against a blue sky.

Cobble together a tree house in your backyard: In times of economic duress, they serve as affordable country homes.

Make tutti-frutti ice cream; it's a sublimely colorful, old-fashioned birthday treat.

### TUTTI-FRUTTI

*To 2 quarts of rich cream add 1 pound of pulverized sugar and 4 eggs well beaten; mix together well, then place on the fire, stirring constantly until brought to the boiling point. Remove immediately and continue to stir until cold. Add vanilla to taste, place in a freezer and when about half frozen mix thoroughly into it 1 pound of preserved fruits in equal parts of peaches, cherries, pineapple, orange, banana, etc. All these fruits are to be cut into small pieces and mixed well with the frozen cream. Mix a color in this, so it will be in veins like marble.*

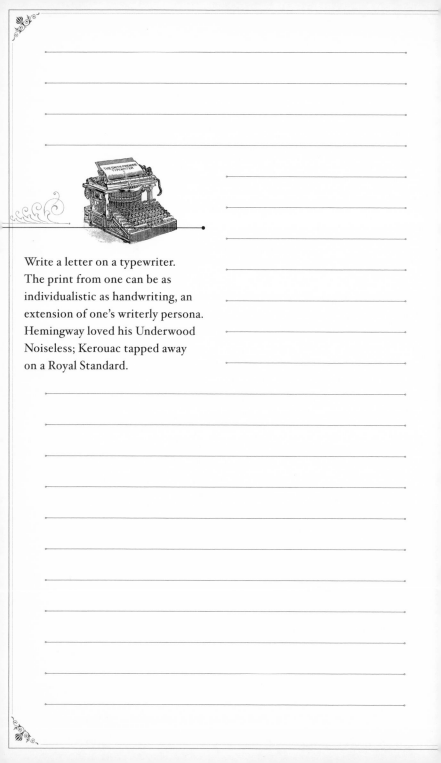

Write a letter on a typewriter. The print from one can be as individualistic as handwriting, an extension of one's writerly persona. Hemingway loved his Underwood Noiseless; Kerouac tapped away on a Royal Standard.

Use the funny
word *underdrawers*.
An equally amusing
synonym: *scanties*.

Set up a vanity table in your bedroom. New York *grande dame* Nan Kempner used to say that the best part of a party was getting ready. Vanity tables make that ritual much more luxurious than raking on makeup in front of a bathroom mirror.

Cultivate a few vices.
Who wouldn't rather
be Scarlett O'Hara
than Melanie Wilkes?

Host a "walking dinner" with your friends: a boisterous old-time Southern take on the potluck dinner whereby a single dinner party would be given at several different houses. Drinks at the first house, appetizers at the next, and so on.

Wallpaper the inside of your car, like they used to do to their "horseless carriages" in the early 1900s. After all, so many people practically live in their cars these days; this might be a very civilized touch.

Track down some wax lips. And while you're at it, try to find other such childhood pleasures, like wax cola bottles, candy cigarettes, bubblegum cigars, Atomic Fireballs, Fun Dip, and Lik-a-Stix.

Use the phrase "Well, I never!"
A good, old-fashioned response
to hearing surprising information,
usually in a gossip scenario, and
a wonderful alternative to the
popularly exclaimed reactive
phrases, "Shut up!" or "No way!"

Take a moment to appreciate Mae West. Once Old Hollywood's Queen of Sassy One-Liners, she uttered quips that are still famous today, such as: "Good girls go to heaven. Bad girls go everywhere else."

Fasten an old-fashioned wicker basket to your bicycle. They look best filled with freshly cut flowers and other farmers' market goodies.

Tell a good old "yarn":
A tall tale, an outlandish
fib of a story.

Have a winter picnic. Bring red plaid blankets and the family dog and stick a bottle of champagne or white wine in the snow to chill it. True intrepids will also cart along a wind-up record player, with old phonographs to echo across the snowy fields.

ISBN: 978-1-4521-0529-1

Manufactured in China

DESIGNED BY SUPRIYA KALIDAS, BASED ON
*LET'S BRING BACK* BOOK DESIGN BY TRACY SUNRISE JOHNSON

ILLUSTRATIONS BY GRADY MCFERRIN

10 9 8 7 6 5 4 3 2

Chronicle Books LLC
680 Second Street
San Francisco, CA 94107

WWW.CHRONICLEBOOKS.COM